This book belongs to the
Cape Vincent Community Library
157 N. Real St.
Cape Vincent, NY 13618

A Mink, a Fink, a Skating Rink

What Is a Noun?

noun: A word that names a person, animal, place, or thing.

A Mink, a Fink, a Skating Rink

What Is a Noun?

by Brian P. Cleary

illustrated by Jenya Prosmitsky

CAROLRHODA BOOKS, INC. / MINNEAPOLIS

Hill
is a
noun.
Mill
is a
noun.

In fact, our whole hometown is a noun.

NOUNS can sometimes
be quite proper,

Like
Brooklyn Bridge,

or

Edward
Hopper,

A jail,
a nail,
a bale of hay,
The pool or park in
Which you play,

A quarter, a porter,
a pencil, or pear—

Nouns are seen
most everywhere.

A box, a lip,

a chocolate chip,

A cup or glass from which you sip,

A pocket, button,
sleeve, or cuff—

A noun can simply
be your stuff.

A mink, a fink, a skating rink,

A cake, a rake, your kitchen sink,

The pope,
some soap

that's on a rope,

A downtown mall,
a downhill slope.

A
house,
a mouse,
a broken
clock,

WELCOME
TO
SANTA FE

New
Mexico,
an old white
sock,

Some tar,
a bar,

a baseball star,

The place where Mother parks her car.

RESERVED for MOM

A noun
can be your
Auntie Lynn,

The mayor of the town you're in,

Your friend
who tells
you corny
jokes—

A noun can be
your favorite folks.

A collar,
a scholar,
a handful
of sand,

Saxes and faxes,
the brass in the band,

A cat, a bat,
your grandma's hat—

Nouns are a little
of this and that.

If it's a place of any kind—

A mountain, hall,
or Highway 9,

A **king**,
a **queen**,
some
gasoline,

A red raspberry
ice **machine**.

If it's a person, place, or thing—

Your dad, Detroit, a diamond ring,

If it's a boat or coat or clown,

It's simple, Simon, it's a noun!

ABOUT THE AUTHOR & ILLUSTRATOR

BRIAN P. CLEARY is the author of several other picture books, including <u>Hairy, Scary, Ordinary: What Is an Adjective?</u> and <u>Give Me Bach My Schubert</u>. He lives in Cleveland, Ohio.

JENYA PROSMITSKY grew up and studied art in Kishinev, Moldova, and lives in Minneapolis. Her two cats, Henry and Freddy, were vital to her illustrations for this book and for <u>Hairy, Scary, Ordinary: What Is an Adjective?</u>

To Molly, Matt, and Andy—three very proper nouns
—B.P.C.

To my mom, who has always been crazy about cats, and my dad, who surprised me by bringing home a kitten when I was 10
—J.P.

Copyright © 1999 by Carolrhoda Books, Inc.

All rights reserved. International copyright secured. No part of this book may be reproduced, stored in a retrieval system, or transmitted in any form or by any means—electronic, mechanical, photocopying, recording, or otherwise—without the prior written permission of Carolrhoda Books, Inc., except for the inclusion of brief quotations in an acknowledged review.

This book is available in two editions:
Library binding by Carolrhoda Books, Inc., a division of Lerner Publishing Group
Soft cover by First Avenue Editions, an imprint of Lerner Publishing Group
241 First Avenue North, Minneapolis, MN 55401 U.S.A.

Website address: www.lernerbooks.com

Library of Congress Cataloging-in-Publication Data

Cleary, Brian P., 1959—
  A mink, a fink, a skating rink : what is a noun? / by Brian P. Cleary ;
illustrated by Jenya Prosmitsky.
    p. cm — (Words are categorical)
  Summary: Rhyming text and illustrations of comical cats present numerous examples of nouns, from "gown" and "crown" to "boat," "coat," and "clown."
  ISBN 1-57505-402-7 (lib. bdg. : alk. paper)
  ISBN 1-57505-417-5 (pbk. : alk. paper)
  1. English language—Noun—Juvenile literature. [1. English language—Noun.] I. Prosmitsky, Jenya, 1974—, ill. II. Title.
III. Series: Cleary, Brian P., 1959— Words are categorical.
PE1201.C58 1999   98—46384
428.2—dc21

Manufactured in the United States of America
4 5 6 7 8 9 — JR — 06 05 04 03 02 01

Find Out More

Books

Gibbs, Maddie. *Jellyfish*. New York: PowerKids Press, 2014.

Magby, Meryl. *Jellyfish*. New York: PowerKids Press, 2013.

Sexton, Colleen. *The Box Jellyfish*. Minneapolis: Bellwether Media, 2012.

Visit this Scholastic Web site for more information on jellyfish:
www.factsfornow.scholastic.com
Enter the keyword **Jellyfish**

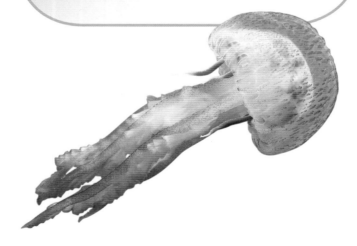

Index

Page numbers in *italics* indicate a photograph or map.

About the Author

Katie Marsico is the author of more than 100 children's books. She was actually stung by a jellyfish in the Caribbean. Fortunately, she survived—and still thinks jellyfish are beautiful and amazing animals.

OCEAN COUNTY LIBRARY

3 3 5 0 0 0 0 4 7 7 9 3 9 3

12
14

BEACHWOOD BRANCH

Ocean County Library
126 Beachwood Blvd
Beachwood, NJ 08722